Mel Bay Presents
The Sal Salvador Jazz Guitar Series

Chordal Enrichment & Chord Substitution

By Sal Salvador
Edited by Joseph J. Roda

The purpose of this series of books is to bring the player from student to pro status. If this book is studied carefully, page by page, I believe this goal can be achieved.

Sal Salvador

*A special appendix entitled "The Jazz Players Handbook" is included on page 65.

© 1985 BY MEL BAY PUBLICATIONS, INC., PACIFIC, MO.
INTERNATIONAL COPYRIGHT SECURED. ALL RIGHTS RESERVED. PRINTED IN U.S.A.

CHORDAL ENRICHMENT AND CHORD SUBSTITUTION
FOR CHORD PLAYING OR IMPROVISING

Editor
Joseph J. Roda

by Sal Salvador

What are the rules of chordal enrichment and substitution? Well, if you're playing by yourself you can do almost anything; but if you want work professionally with groups, in studios, etc., whatever you play has to be compatible with what other musicians play or the consequences will have a very negative effect on your career as a musician. As you grow musically, you will come to realize that there is a common musical language that enables professional players to create together. The rules set forth in this book should culminate in the ability to communicate musically in any given situation.

EXTENSIONS AND ALTERATIONS

An important rule to remember is a jazz player should not use a plain major chord (1, 3, 5) or a plain dominant 7th chord (1, 3, 5, lowered 7) expect for effect. These chords sound out of context in jazz. This is where the use of extensions and alterations comes into play.

I. Major Chords (1, 3, 5)

The <u>extension</u> is the basic chord with one or more scale tones added, such as: the basic C chord can become:

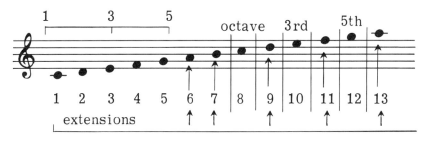

Key of C major
| 1 3 5 |

C6 = 1 3 5 6
     C E G A

Cmaj.7 = 1 3 5 7
        C E G B

Cmaj.9 = 1 3 5 7 9   Cmaj.7 add 13 = 1 3 5 7 13
        C E G B D   C E G B A

Cmaj.7 add $\frac{6}{9}$ = 1 3 5 6 7 9   C6 add 9 = 1 3 5 6 9
               C E G A B D   C E G A D

C add 9 = 1 3 5 9   Cmaj.9 add 13 = 1 3 5 7 9 13
        C E G D   C E G B D A

2

the basic F chord can becomes

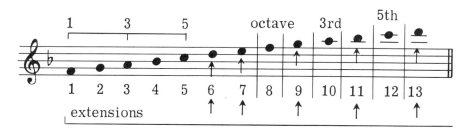

Key of F major
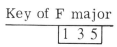

F6 - 1 3 5 6
   F A C D

Fmaj.7 - 1 3 5 7
     F A C E

Fmaj.9 - 1 3 5 7 9
     F A C E G

Fmaj.7 add $^6_9$ - 1 3 5 6 7 9
         F A C D E G

F add 9 - 1 3 5 9
     F A C G

Fmaj.7 add 13 - 1 3 5 7 13
        F A C E D

F6 add 9 - 1 3 5 6 9
     F A C D G

Fmaj.9 add 13 - 1 3 5 7 9 13
       F A C E G D

the basic B♭ chord can become

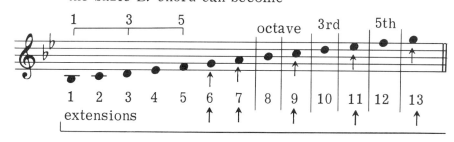

Key of B♭ major
1 3 5

B♭6 - 1 3 5 6
   B♭ D F G

B♭maj.7 - 1 3 5 7
     B♭ D F A

B♭maj.9 - 1 3 5 7 9
     B♭ D F A C

B♭maj.7 add $^6_9$ - 1 3 5 6 7 9
        B♭ D F G A C

B♭add 9 - 1 3 5 9
     B♭ D F C

B♭ maj.7 add 13 - 1 3 5 7 13
        B♭ D F A G

B♭6 add 9 - 1 3 5 6 9
     B♭ D F G C

B♭maj.9 add 13 - 1 3 5 7 9 13
       B♭ D F A C G

Notice the 7th (natural or flatted) must be present to determine whether a chord is major or dominant. Also, if the chord is a 9th, 11th, or 13th, this implies the 7th is present. If not, the 13th would be a 6th.

Here are some common forms that should be learned.

FORM I (Root on the 6th string)

These inversions can be played on different frets to get the chords in different keys.

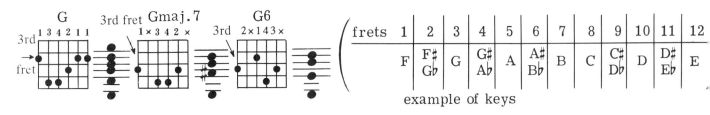

These examples can be used to enrich a plain major, such as G for 2 measures.

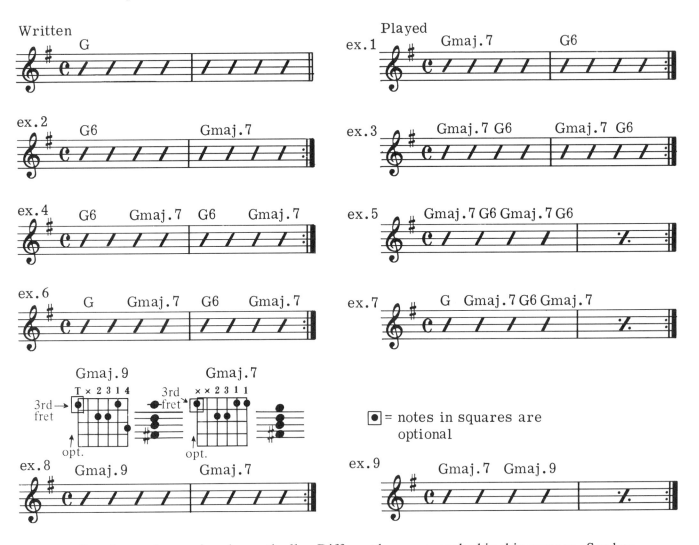

Practice each exercise chromatically. Different keys are reached in this manner. See key example above.

4

FORM II (root on the 5th string)

These inversions can be played on different frets to get the chords in different keys.

Example of keys

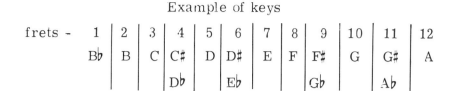

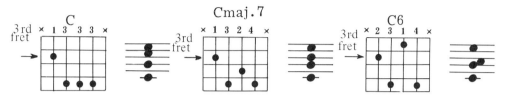

This form should be practiced chromatically as in Form I.

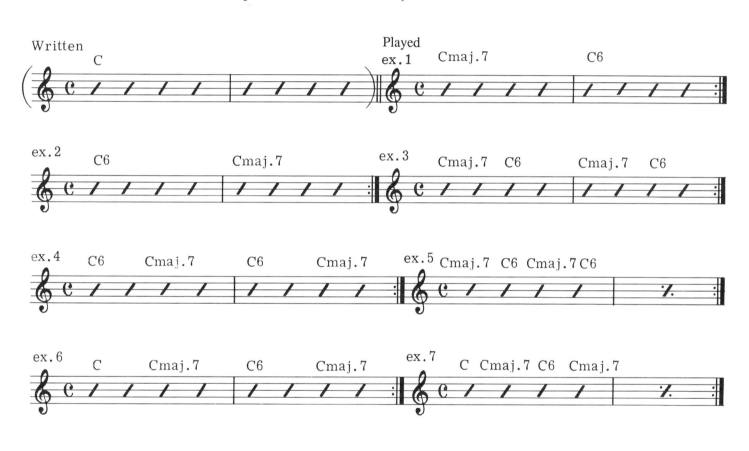

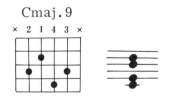

II. Minor Chords (1, ♭3, 5)

Use the same extensions as major chords.

C minor   1 ♭3   5

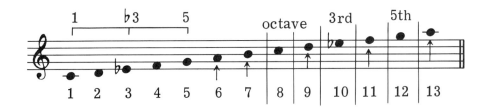

Cm6 = 1 ♭3   5   6

Cm7 = 1 ♭3   5   Lowered 7

Cm add $^6_9$ = 1 ♭3 5 6 9

Cm add maj.7 = 1 ♭3 5 7

Cm11 = 1 ♭3   5   Lowered 7   11

Cm9 = 1 ♭3   5   Lowered 7   9

Cm9(maj.7) = 1 ♭3   5   ♮7   9

Cm7 add 13 = 1 ♭3   5   Lowered 7   (9)   13

Cmadd 9 = 1 ♭3   5   9

Cm9 add 13 = 1 ♭3   5   ♭7   13

Cm9(maj.7) add 13 = 1 ♭3   5   ♮7   9   13

F minor   1 ♭3   5

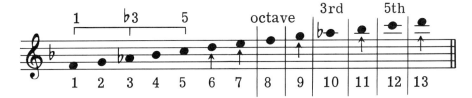

Fm6 = 1 ♭3   5   6

Fm7 = 1 ♭3   5   Lowered 7

Fm add $^6_9$ = 1 ♭3 5 6 9

Fm add maj.7 = 1 ♭3   5   ♮7

Fm11 = 1 ♭3   5   Lowered 7   11

Fm9 = 1 ♭3   5   Lowered 7   9

Fm9 maj.7 = 1 ♭3   5   ♮7   9

Fm.7 add 13 = 1 ♭3   5   Lowered ♭7   (9)   13

Fm add 9 = 1 ♭3   5   9

Fm9 add 13 = 1 ♭3   5   Lowered 7   (9)   13

Fm9(maj.7) add 13 = 1 ♭3   5   ♮7   9   13

B♭ minor 1 ♭3   5

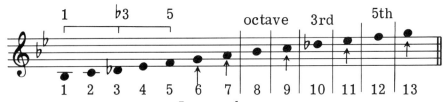

B♭m6 1 ♭3 5 6

B♭m7 1 ♭3 5 Lowered 7

B♭m add $^6_9$ 1 ♭3 5 6 9

B♭m add maj^7 1 ♭3 5 ♮7

B♭m 11 1 ♭3 5 Lowered 7 11

B♭m9 1 ♭3 5 Lowered 7 9

B♭m9 maj.7 1 ♭3 5 ♮7 9

B♭m9 add9 13 1 ♭3 5 Lowered 7 (9) 13

B♭m add 9 1 ♭3 5 9

B♭m9 add 13 1 ♭3 5 Lowered 7 13

B♭m9 maj7 add13 1 ♭3 5 ♮7 9 13

Common minor forms that should be learned. As you learn other forms feel free to use them according to your own musical tastes.

FORM I (root on the 6th string)

III. Dominant 7th chords (1, 3, 5, ♭7)

Dominant 7th chords always have a lowered 7th. and use the same extensions as both the major and minor chords.

C7 = 1 3 5 Lowered 7

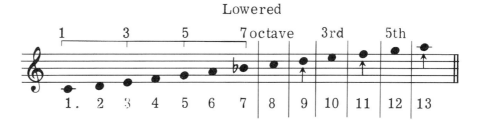

C9 = 1 3 5 Lowered 9
              7

C13 = 1 3 5 Lowered $\binom{9}{opt.}$ 13
              7

C sus = 1 4 5 ♭7

C11 = 1 3 5 Lowered $\binom{9}{opt.}$ 11
              7

F7 = 1 3 5 Lowered 7

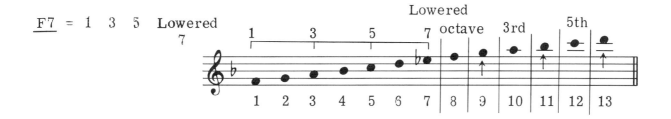

F9 = 1 3 5 Lowered 9
              7

F13 = 1 3 5 Lowered $\binom{9}{opt.}$ 13
              7

F11 = 1 3 5 Lowered $\binom{9}{opt.}$ 11
              7

F sus = 1 4 5 ♭7

B♭7 = 1 3 5 Lowered 7

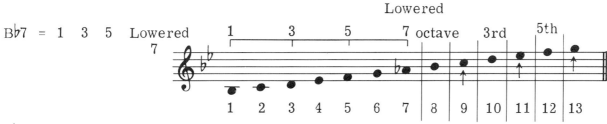

B♭9 = 1 3 5 Lowered 9
              7

B♭11 = 1 3 5 Lowered $\binom{9}{opt.}$ 11
              7

B♭13 = 1 3 5 Lowered $\binom{9}{opt.}$ 13
              7

B♭ sus = 1 4 5 ♭7

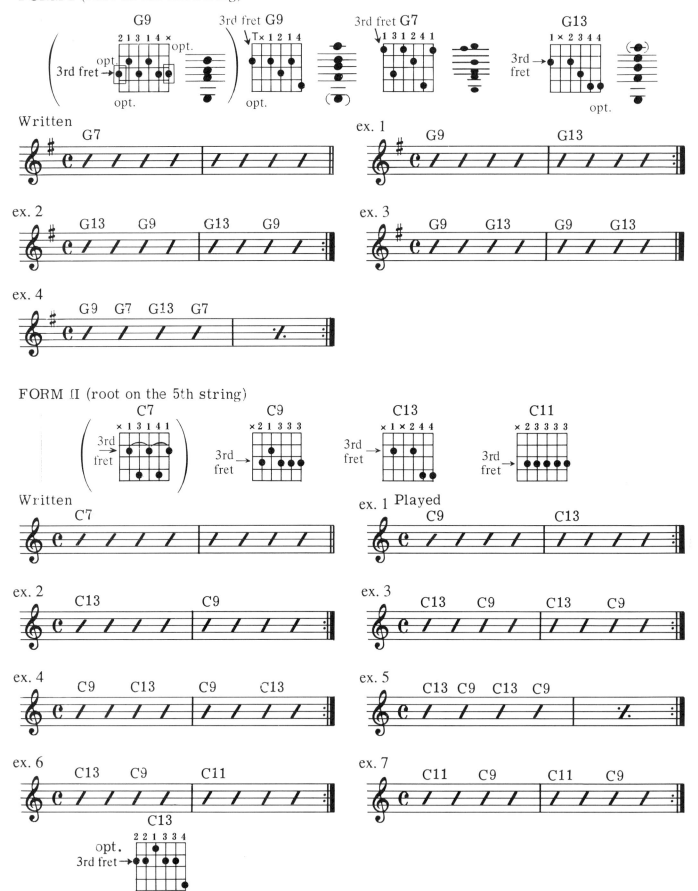

Alterations are any of the previously discussed chords with either 1 or more notes raised or lowered. This is done by adding a sharp, # or flat, ♭.

The alterations can be major or dominant.

Here are some examples. Place the symbols maj, min, min. 7 or dom. 7 before each one.

♭5, #5, ♭9, #9, ♭5♭9, ♭5#9, #5♭9, #5#9, 7♭5, 7#5, 7♭9, 7#9, 7♭5♭9, 7♭5#9, 7#5♭9, 7#5#9, 13♭5, 13#5, 13♭9, 13#9, 13♭5♭9, 13♭5#9, 9♭5, 9#5, 13#5♭9, 13#5#9.

The dominant alterations are used most often.

We will learn these examples first and then add the majors & minors as we go along. (root on the 6th string)

IV. Rules for Chordal Substitution (See Handbook at back of book.)

Now that we've learned some common chordal extensions and alterations, we will start to learn rules for chord substituting.

Rule

The 5 minor 7 of the dominant 7th can be used before, after, or in place of the dominant 7th and its related extensions. For example, when you have G7 for 2 measures you can use the following:

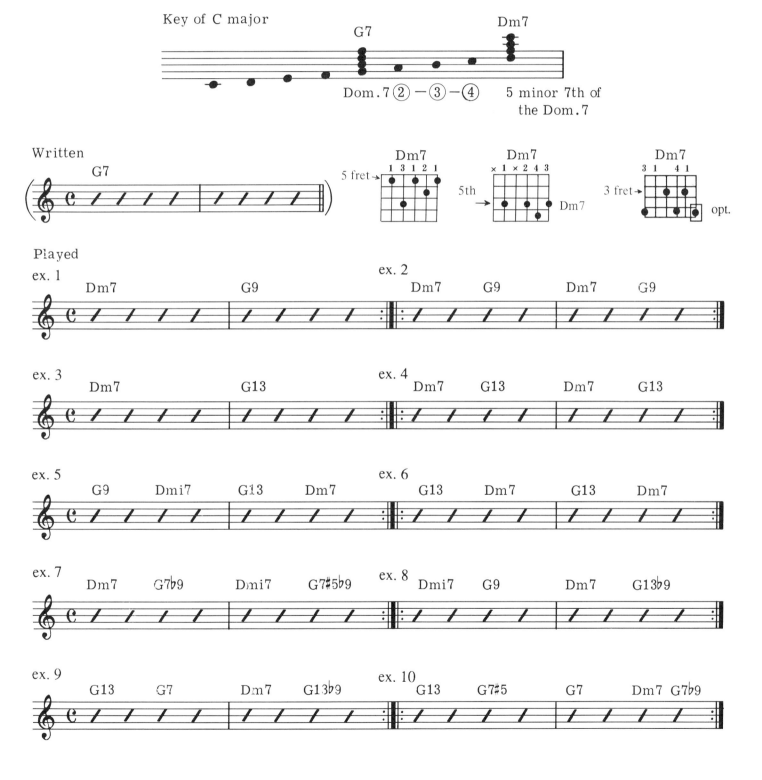

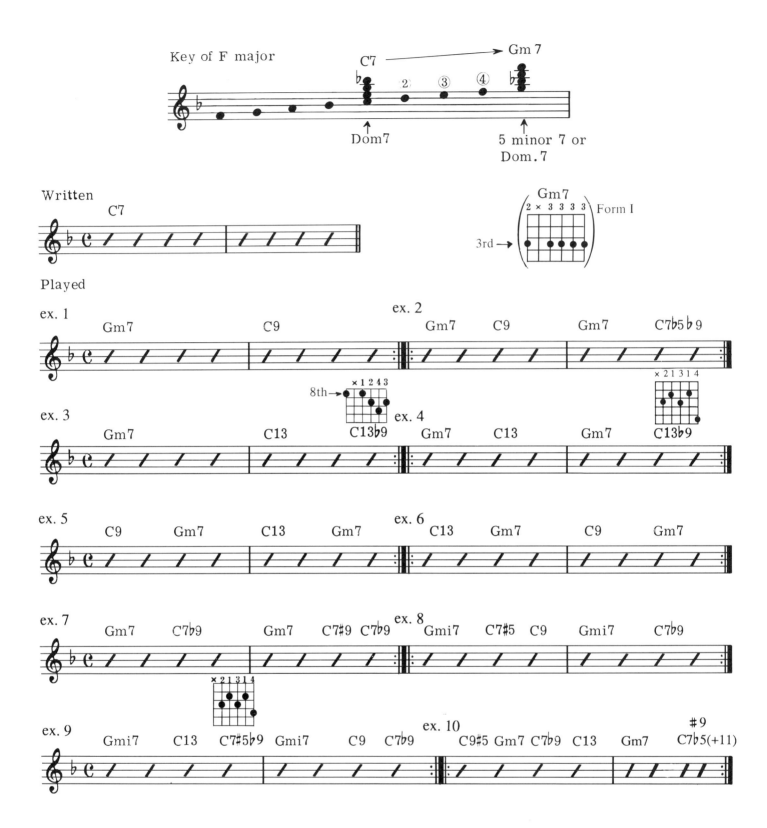

The 2, 5 Progression

Rule

When Dm7 is used before G dom. the 2, 5 progression is created, the Dm7 being the 2 chord of the C major scale and the G dominant (G9, G13, G7♭9, etc.) the 5 chord.

(Notice that the 2 chord is the same as the 5 minor 7th of the dominant 7th discussed earlier.)

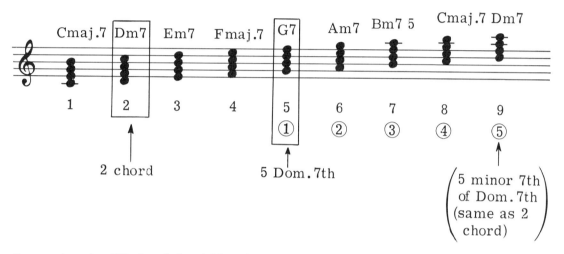

Remember the G7 chord should be altered and extended with the forms we learned:

7♭5, 7♯5, 9, 9♭5, 9♯5, 13, 13♭5, 13♯5, 13♭9, 13♯9, 13♭5♭9, 13♯5♭9, 13♭5♯9, 13♯5♯9, 11.
Notice the bass line moves in 4ths.

Some interesting variations on chords may be obtained by switching a 1st string note to the 6th string or alternately switching a 6th string note to the 1st string. Try this; it will increase your chord color vocabulary.

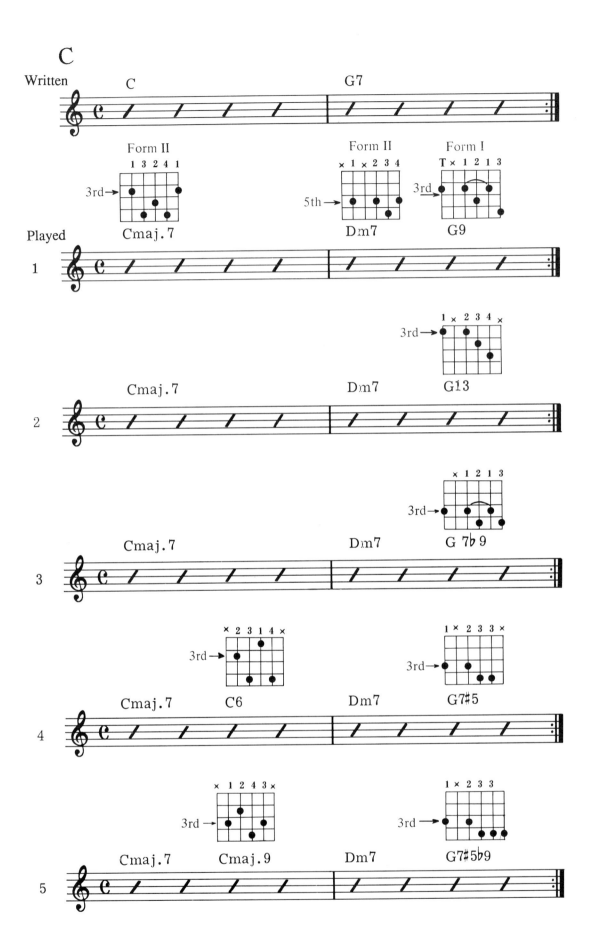

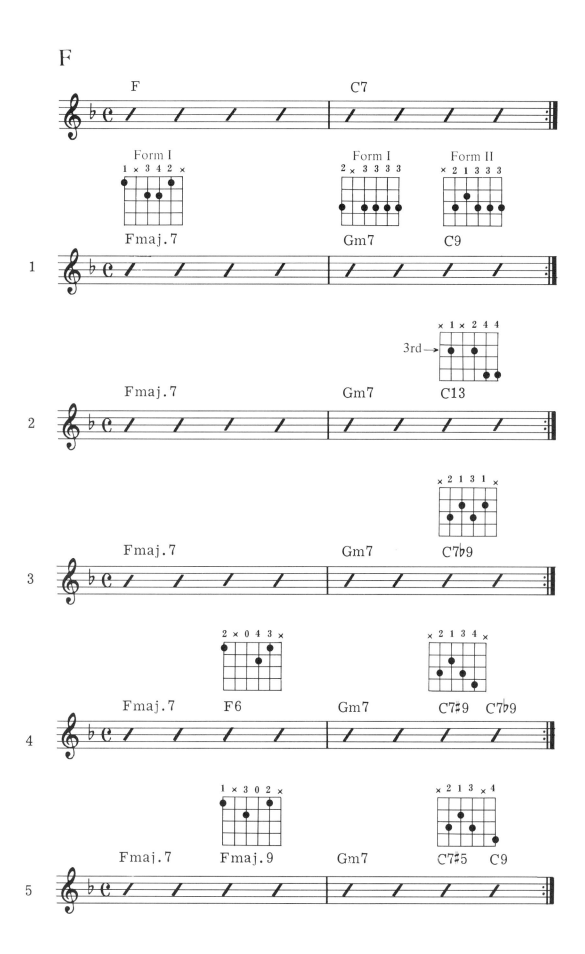

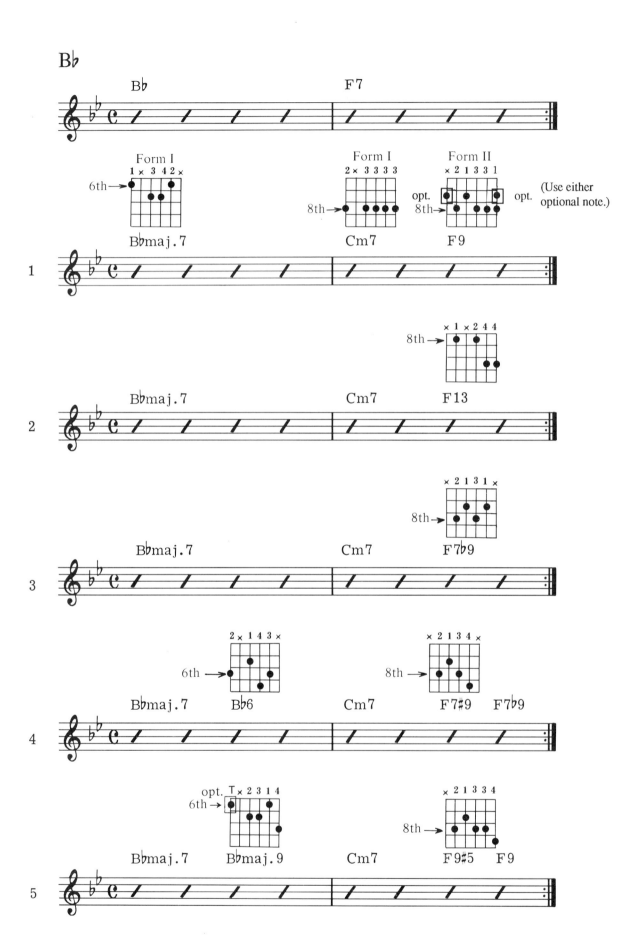

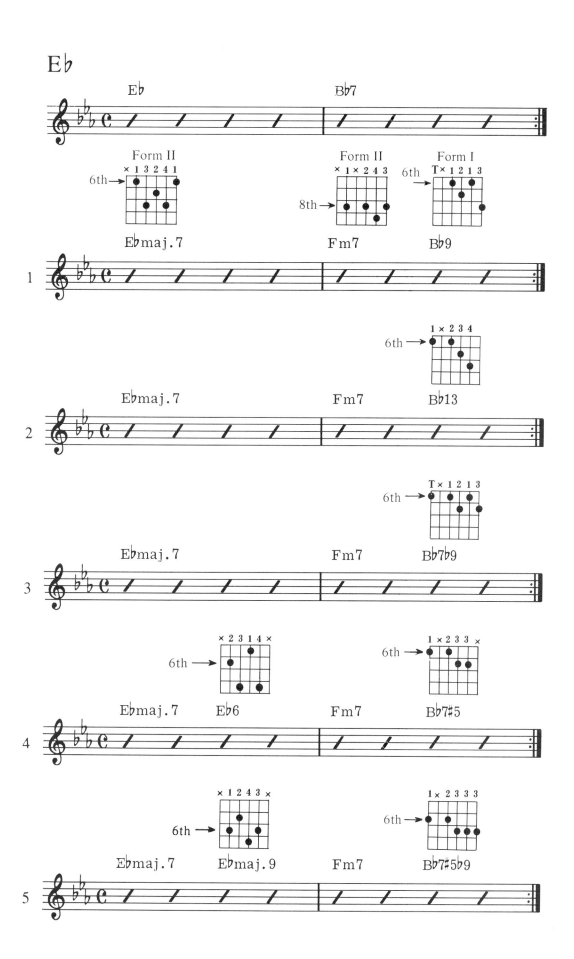

The 3 minor 7 chord and the 6 minor 7 chord can be used in place of the 1 major.
Notice how the minor 7th chords overlap to the next key in the cycle of 4ths.
A valuable improvising tool.

Examples

Key of Cmajor: Em7 (3rd of C)
                                                  > Cmajor
                        Am7 (6th of C)

Key of Fmajor: Am7 (3rd of F)
                                                  > Fmajor
                        Dmi7 (6th of F)

Key of B♭major   Dmi7 (3rd of B♭)
                                                  > B♭major
                        Gm7 (6th of B♭)

Key of E♭major   Gm7 (3rd of E♭)
                                                  > E♭major
                        Cm7 (6th of E♭)

Key of A♭major   Cm7 (3rd of A♭)
                                                  > A♭major
                        Fm7 (6th of A♭)

Key of D♭major   Fm7 (3rd of D♭)
                                                  > D♭major
                        B♭m7 (6th of D♭)

Key of G♭major   B♭m7 (3rd of G♭)
                                                  > G♭major
                        E♭m7 (6th of G♭)

Key of B major   D♯m7 (3rd of B)
                                                  > Bmajor
                        G♯m7 (6th of B)

Key of Emajor   G♯m7 (3rd of E)
                                                  > Emajor
                        C♯m7 (6th of E)

Key of Amajor   C♯m7 (3rd of A)
                                                  > Amajor
                        F♯m7 (6th of A)

Key of Dmajor   F♯m7 (3rd of D)
                                                  > Dmaj.7
                        Bm7 (6th of D)

Key of Gmajor   Bm7 (3rd of G)
                                                  > Gmaj.7
                        Em7 (6th of G)

Rule

The 1, 6, 2, 5 progression is derived from the basic C four beats and G7 four beats. Also, altered  + extended <u>major</u> chords make interesting endings.

Practice these exercises:

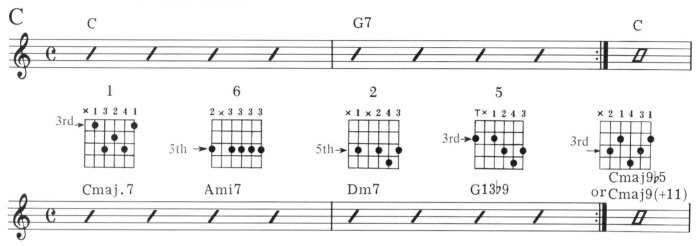

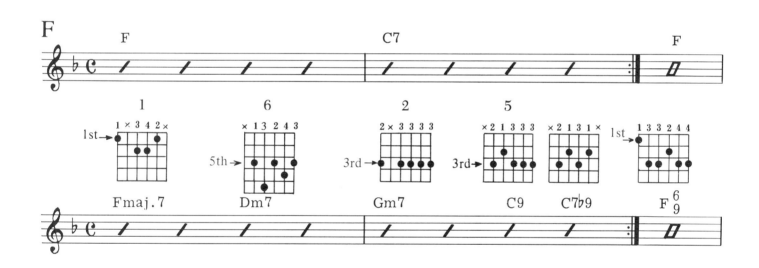

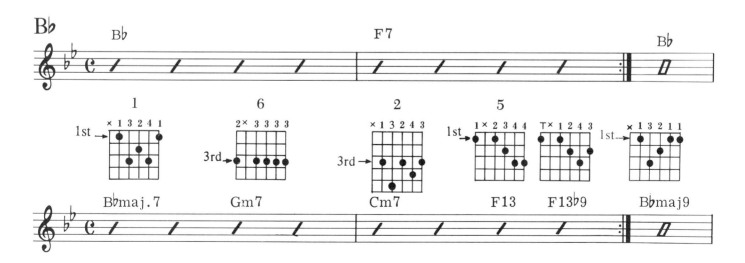

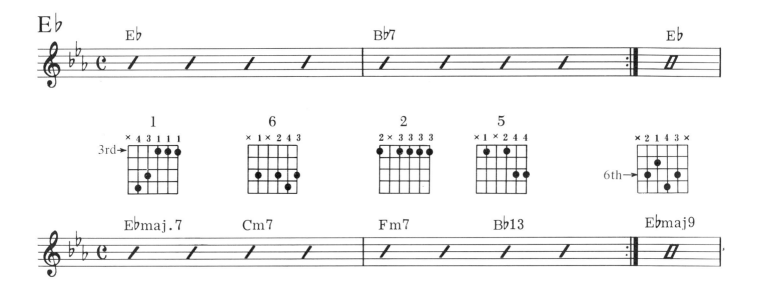
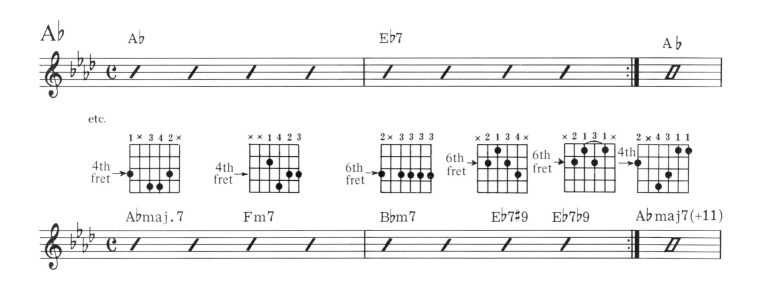
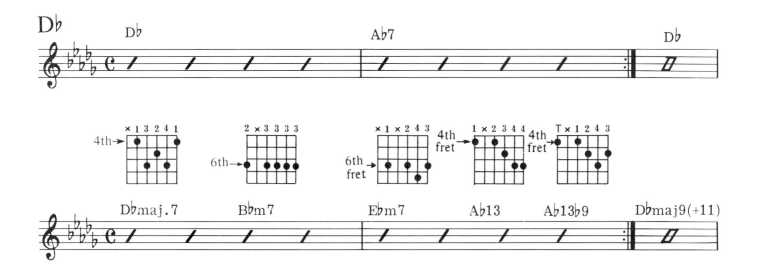

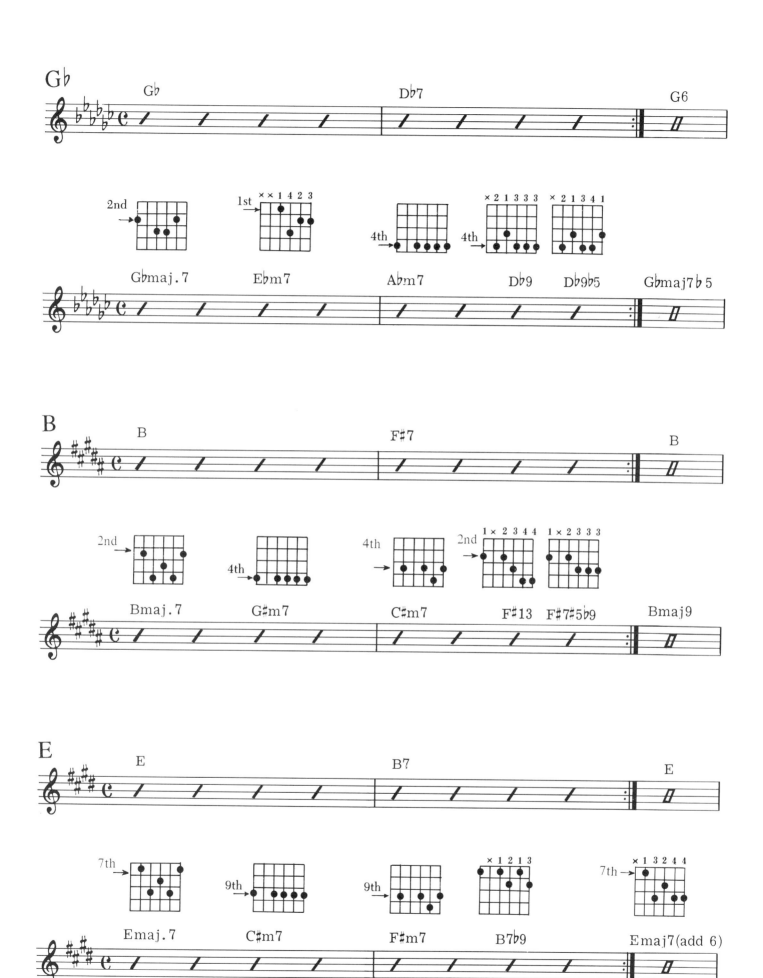

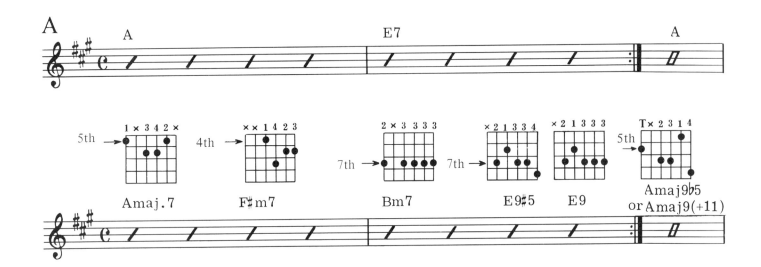
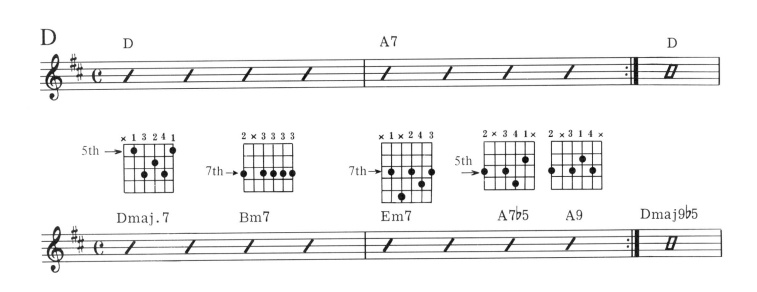
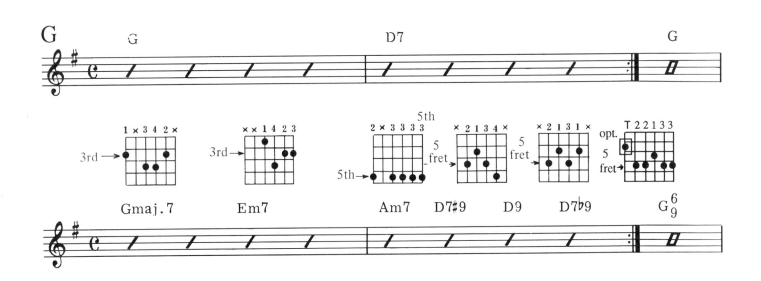

Rule

The 1, 3, 2, 5 progression is not as common as the 1, 6, 2, 5 but it should be practiced in all keys. The 1, 3, 2, 5 progression can be used as a replacement for the 1, 6, 2, 5 progression, in same cases.

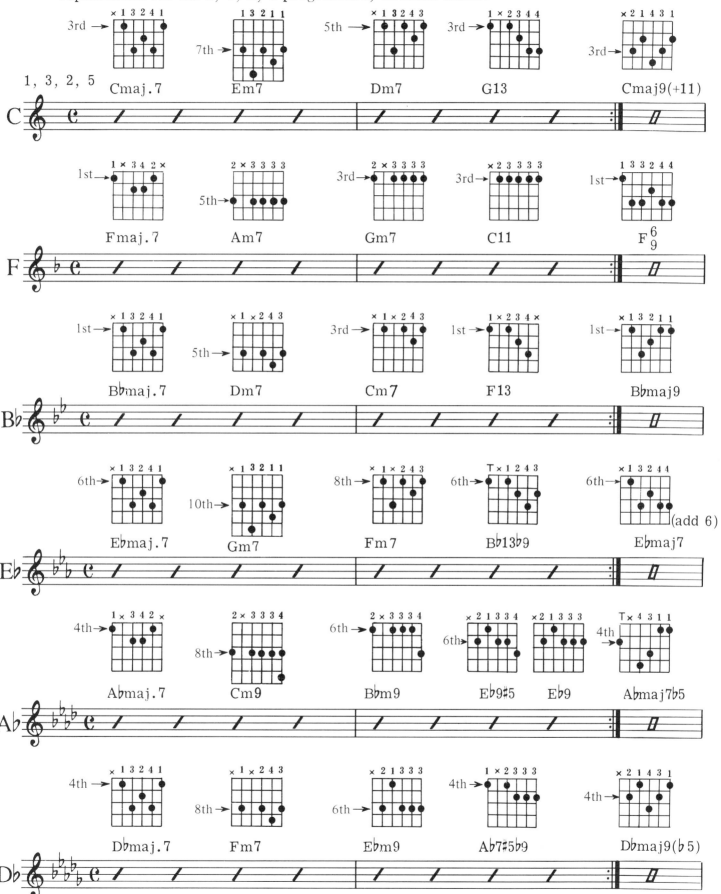

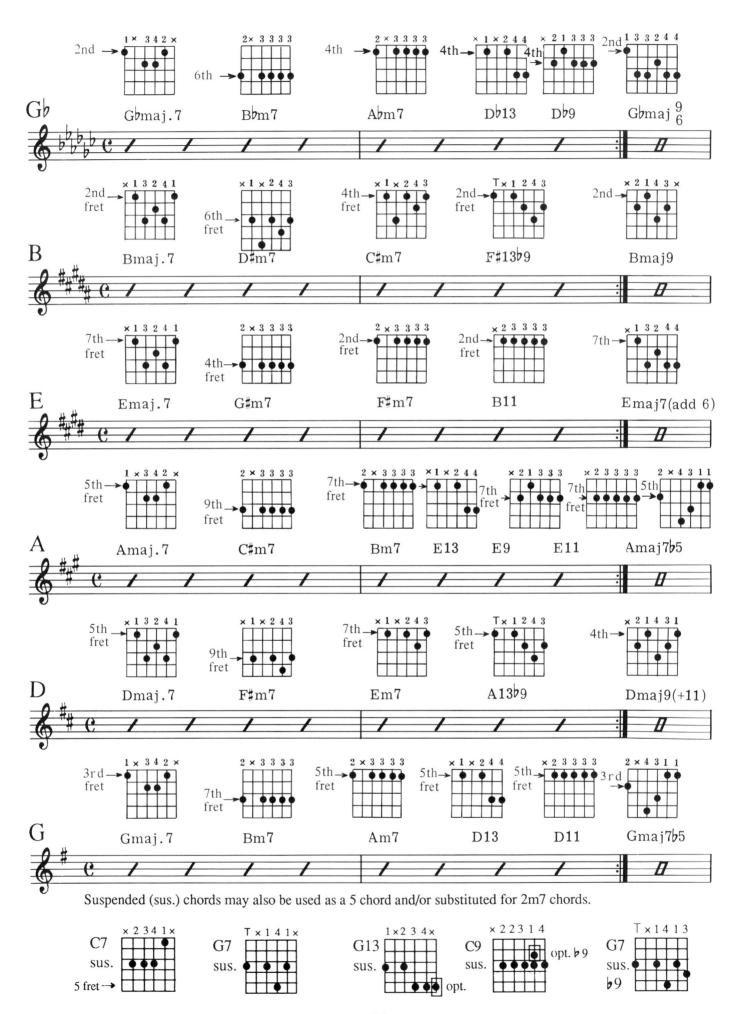

Rule A note about the minor 7th chords. They really belong to the dominant family as they are a 2 chord and like the 5 chord they both lead back to the 1 chord. Both the 5 dom. 7th chord and the 2 minor 7th chord contain the lowered 7th also called minor 7th or dominant 7th. However, you can add to and alter the 2 chord as well as the dominant 7th.

Examples of the altered 2 chord.

Practice these examples: (2, 5, 1, progressions)

I have included some suspended chords in this section. Try using some of your own as explained on p. 30. They sound harmonious especially if you play the sus. first and then drop the 4th (sus. note) to a 3rd. Any 11th chord without a 3rd is a sus. chord.

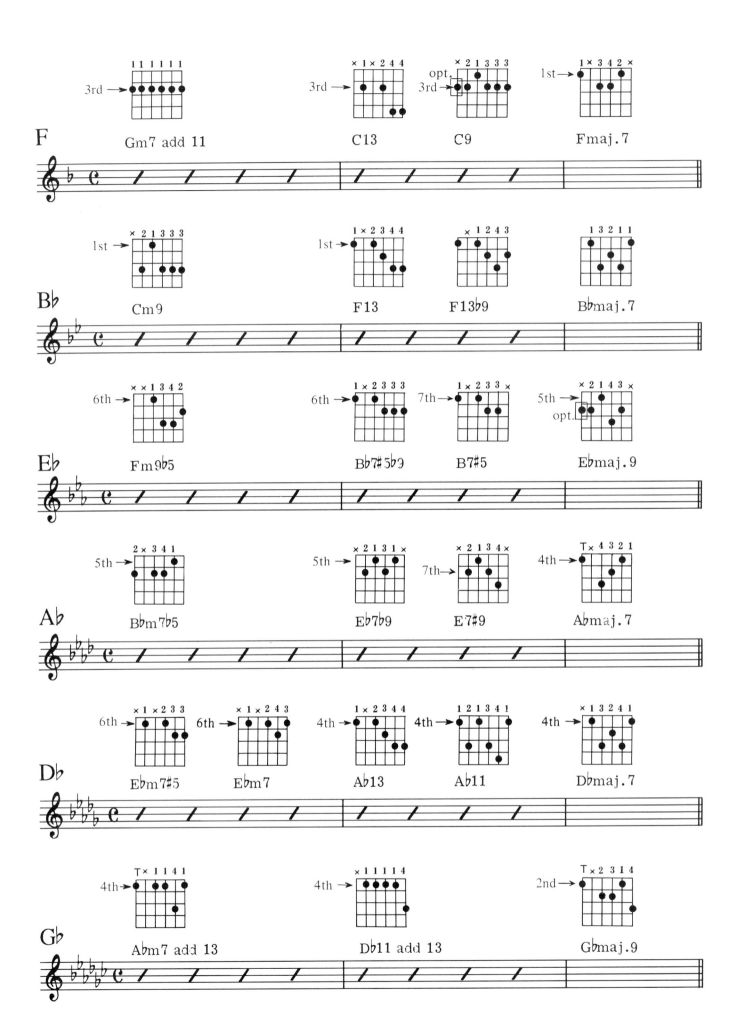

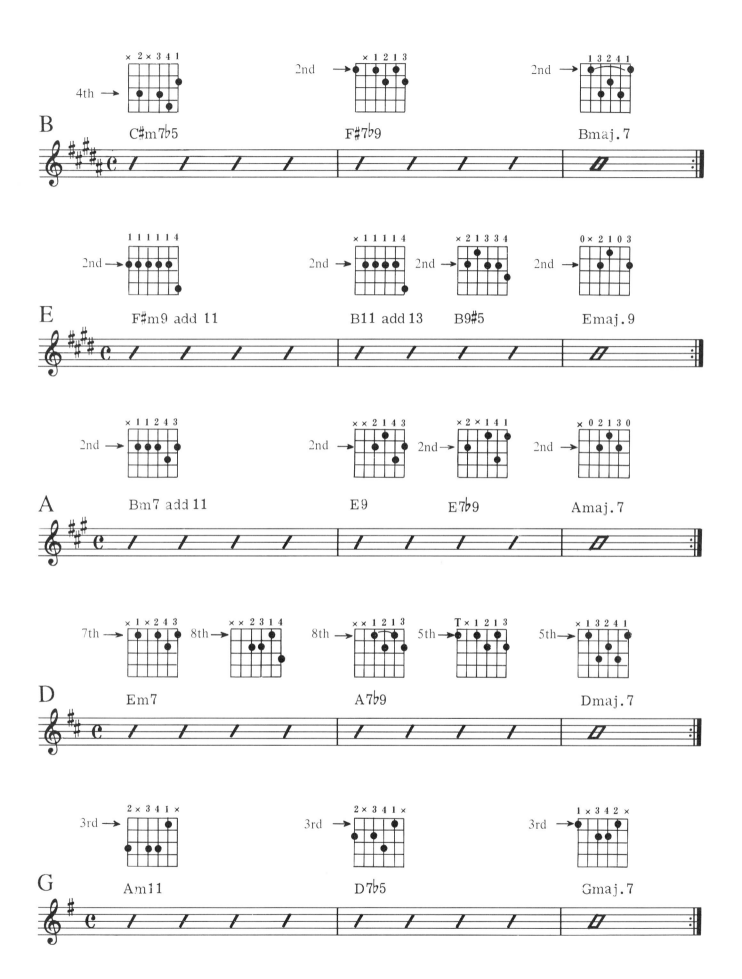

Rule

The flat 5 dominant of the dominant 7th chord can also be used in place of the 5 dominant chord.

example: Key of C major

The flat 5 dominant of the dominant 7th (dominant 7th chord is

ex.— G7 (5 chord))

⑤

①   G7   (A   B   C)   D

         1   2   3   4   5

                     ↑

②   make this D a flat - D♭

③   make D♭ a dominant 7th (D♭7)

④   alter the D♭7. (9, 13, 7♭9, etc.)

Now the D♭7 chord can be used as a substitute for the G7.

original	—	Dm7	G9	—	Cmaj.7
example:		(2)	(♭5 of 5)		(1)
Key of C major		Dm7	D♭9		Cmaj.7

Notice the bass line moves chromatically.

The ♭5 dom. substitute of 5 dom. should be altered and extended.

Practice these examples:

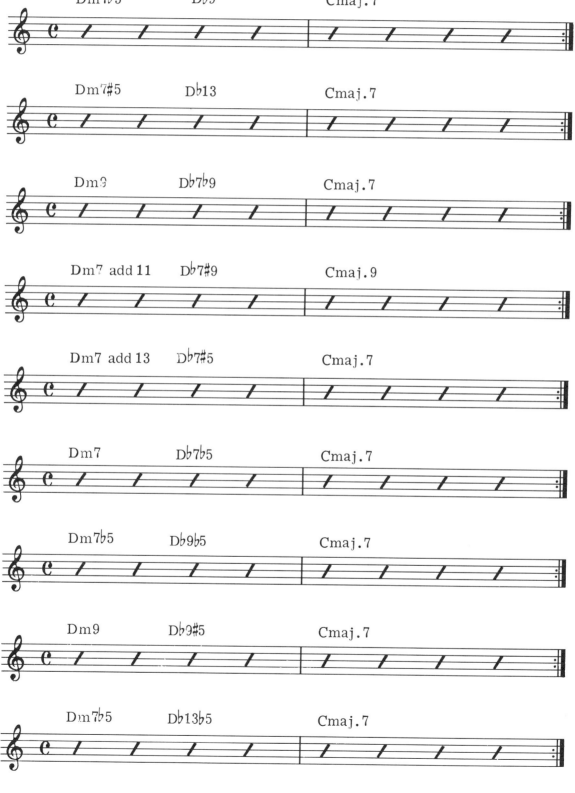

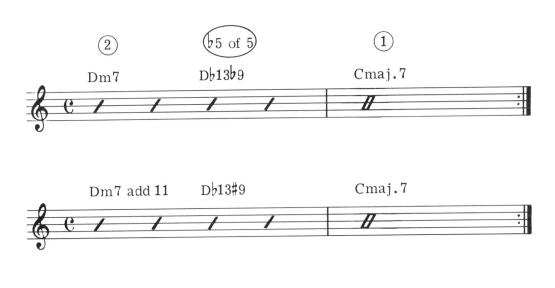

Rule

This is also called the tri-tone substitution. The tri-tone is the interval of an augmented 4th (or a diminished 5th). The name is derived from counting 3 whole tones from

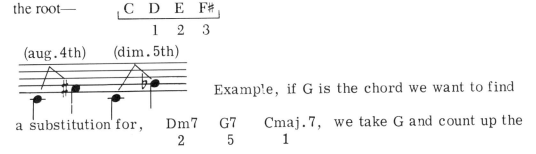

Example, if G is the chord we want to find a substitution for, Dm7 G7 Cmaj.7, we take G and count up the 2 5 1

tri-tone (aug. 4th or diminished 5th) this will become D♭ dom. (the ♭5 of 5.)

Practice these examples:

Key of C

Rule

When you see a minor 6th chord leading to a dominant 7th chord, one whole tone above (Gm6 to A7 9), it is misspelled. It should be called the 5 minor 7th flat 5 of the dominant 7th chord. (Em7♭5 to A7♭9) this creates the 2, 5, 1, progression in minor.

Practice these examples:

Now it is time to combine some of the rules we have learned. This, you will find, will offer unlimited possibilities of chordal substitution. Remember the 5 minor 7th = dom. 7th. If you are using G7♭9 to Cm7 of even Cmaj.7, try placing the 5 minor 7th of the dominant before it and alter that, too. Another example of this is an original change like:

You could place the <u>altered</u> dominant 7th on the 2 beats before the Cm7 to lead into it.

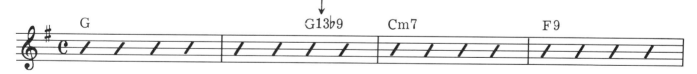

Now place the 5 minor 7 substitution before the G13♭9.

Rule

When leading to a minor (3rd) type chord, <u>always</u> alter the dominant 7th before it. You will hear the difference. Play and listen to the difference between G9 to Cm and G7♭9 to Cm. Alter or extend any plain chords.

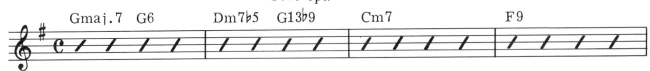

To go a step further, use the E minor 7 substitution of G in the 1st bar creating the sound of coming down the C scale from 3, 2, to 5 dominant.

Or do the reverse by going up the G scale.

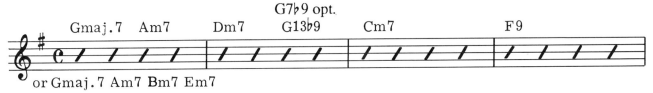

or Gmaj.7 Am7 Bm7 Em7

You may also add altered dominant 7th chords or more minor 7th chords.

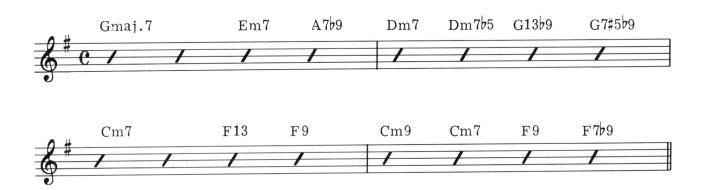

Quite different from the original.

40

Now we will take the same progression and add some more of these moves so that you can see how many ways they can be varied.

Let's work only with the 1st 2 measures.

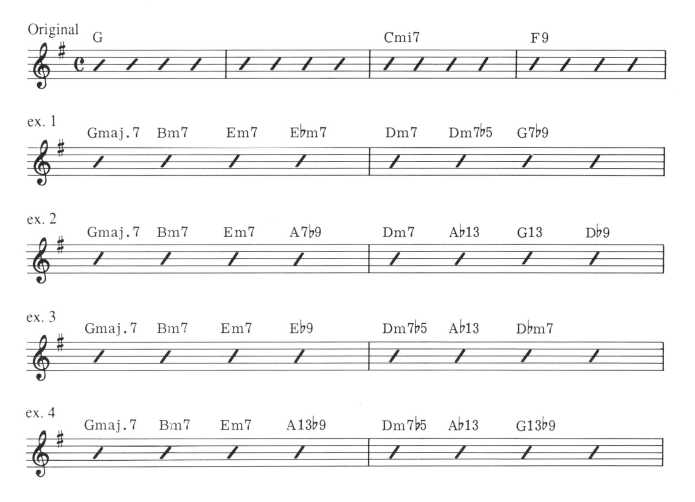

Again for the more adventuresome we can use the ♭5 substitutions and chromatic moves to further enhance this progression.

The chromatic moves can come from below or above the original chord.

G♭13 to G13 or A♭13 to G13, Dm7 to D♯m7 or Em7 to E♭m7, Gm7 to G♯m7 or Am7 to G♯m7 (a minor 3rd move with jazz is replete) it can become.

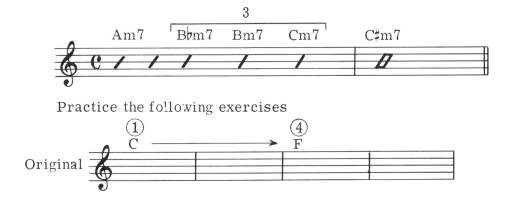

Practice the following exercises

41

Rule

I would like to reiterate, use a 7th flat 9 chord instead of a diminished chord.

example:

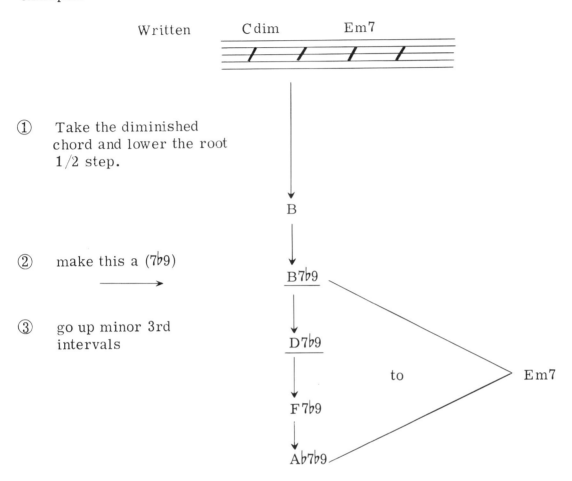

① Take the diminished chord and lower the root 1/2 step.

② make this a (7♭9)

③ go up minor 3rd intervals

④ You now have 4 choices of 7♭9 chords to place before the Em7 (in place of Cdim.) pick the most logical B7♭9 (5 of Em7) or any of the others, depending on the sound your looking for. You will usually find 2 (♭5 tritone subs of each other) that are sonorous and 2 that are not. As seen here, once you've made the basic substitution you can then proceed to add alterations or extensions to the substitute.

Remember, with each diminished chord you have a choice of 4 dom. 7♭9 chords. Always play all of your choices first, as with all these rules, then pick the substitution you like—keep the melody in mind and use your ear!! If you don't do that, the whole thing is a waste of time. Music must be played with feeling, hearing (or soul and ears), and imagination, or it comes out computerized. I have yet to hear a computer swing or create a jazz or soul feeling with human overtones.

Remember that <u>any</u> chord with a lowered 7th in it is a leading chord and any chord with a major 7th (natural 7) stops the harmony.

The 2 minor 7th or the 5 dom. 7th chord will determine the tonal center. Dm7 and G dom. are in the key of C major when both the 2 chord and the 5 dom. chord are altered. This usually means the tonal center is minor, although the two altered chords <u>could</u> lead to major.

ex. (Dm7♭5 to G7♭9 to Cm) or Dm7♭5 G7♭9 to C69

or $\begin{smallmatrix} 3 & 2 & 1 & 1 & 3 & 3 \\ T & T & 1 & 1 & 3 & 3 \end{smallmatrix}$

Many chords that have the same notes become different chords when they are used with different bass notes. Chords can also change identity when placed in progressions in unusual ways.

Rules:

1) C6 = Am7

Any major 6 chord will have the same notes as a minor 7th chord (a 6th higher or a minor 3rd lower)

2) Cm6 = Am7♭5

a minor 6th chord can be replaced by a minor 7th♭5 (a 6th higher or a minor 3rd lower)

3) Cmaj.7 = Am9

a maj.7 chord can be replaced by a min.9th chord a 6th higher or a minor 3rd lower.

4) Cm (add maj.7) = G+

a minor (add maj.7) chord can be used in place of an augmented chord a 5th higher or a 4th lower.

Other chords that have the same notes.

C6 = Am7	Cmaj.7 = Am9
Cm6 = Am7♭5	Cm(maj.7) = G+
F6 = Dm7	Fmaj.7 = Dm9
Fm6 = Dm7♭5	Fm(maj.7) = C+
B♭6 = Gm7	B♭maj.7 = Gm9
B♭m6 = Gm7♭5	B♭m(maj.7) = F+

G6 = C maj. 9 (no root)

Minor third intervals also play an important role in substituting.

Diminished chords and diminished 7th chords along with 7♭9 chords repeat themselves in minor 3rds.

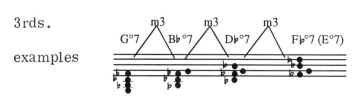

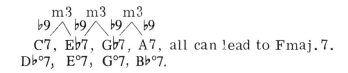

C7, E♭7, G♭7, A7, all can lead to Fmaj.7.
D♭°7, E°7, G°7, B♭°7.

Practice the following examples in all keys.

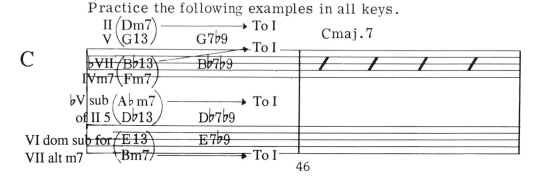

F

Gm7 C9	C7b9	Fmaj.7
Bbm7Eb9	Eb7b9	
Dbm7Gb9	Gb7b9	
Em7 A9	A7b9	

Bb

Cm7 F13	F7b9	Bbmaj.7
Ebm7Ab13	Ab7b9	
F#m7 B13	B7b9	
Am7 D13	D7b9	

Eb

Fm7 Bb9	Bb13	Ebmaj.7
Abm7 Db9	Db13	
Bm7 E9	E13	
Dm7 G9	G13	

Ab

Bbm7Eb13 Eb7b9	Abmaj.7
Dbm7Gb13 Gb7b9	
Em7A13 A7b9	
Gm7C13 C7b9	

Db

Ebm7Ab13 Ab7b9	Dbmaj.7
Gbm7Cb13 Cb7b9	
Am7D13 D7b9	
Cm7F13 F7b9	

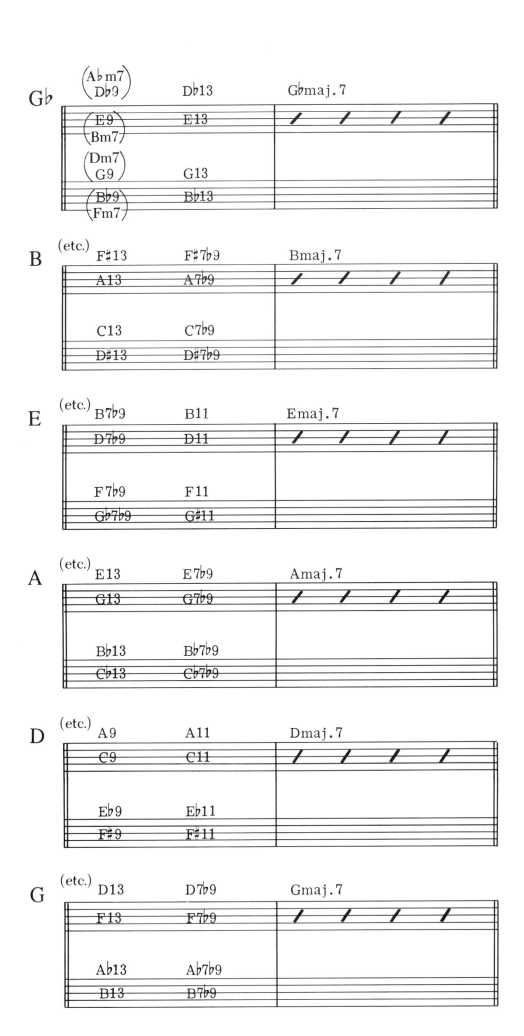

This principle also holds true with the minor 7th chords. Their function is the same as a 5dom. 7th.

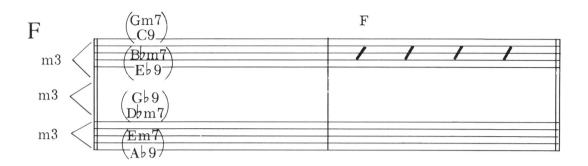

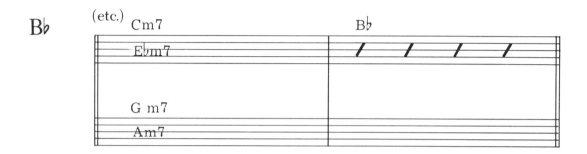

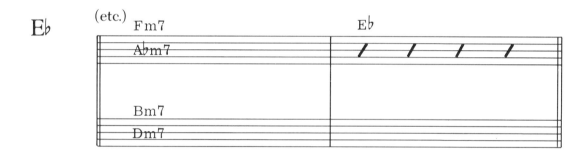

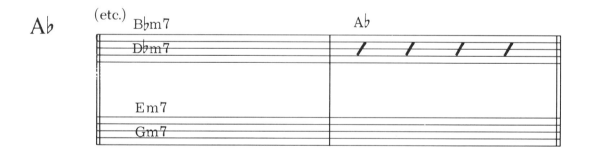

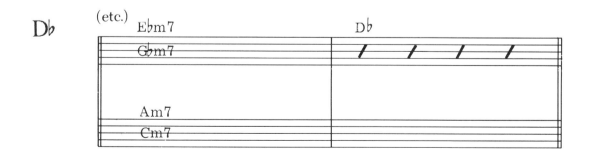

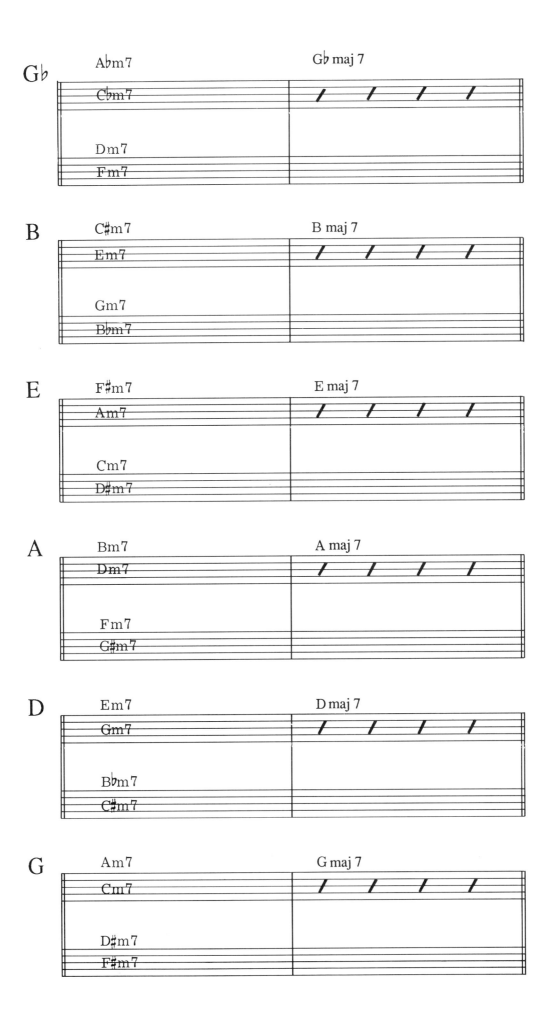

Major 7th chords can move in minor 3rds.

C | Dm7 / / / / | Cmaj.7
Ebmaj.7
F#maj.7
Amaj.7

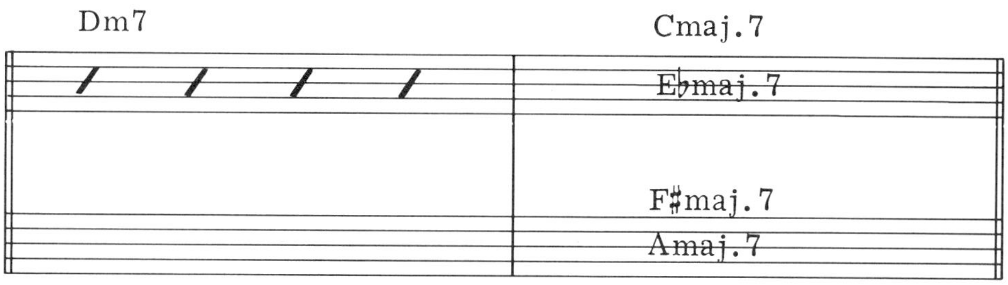

F | Gm7 / / / / | Fmaj.7
Abmaj.7
Bmaj.7
Dmaj.7

Bb | Cm7 / / / / | Bbmaj.7
C#maj.7
Emaj.7
Gmaj.7

Eb | Fm7 / / / / | Ebmaj.7
Gbmaj.7
Amaj.7
Cmaj.7

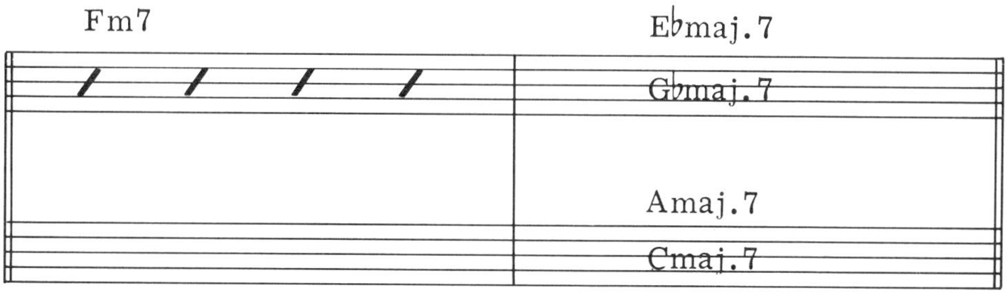

Ab | Bbm7 / / / / | Abmaj.7
Bmaj.7
Dmaj.7
Fmaj.7

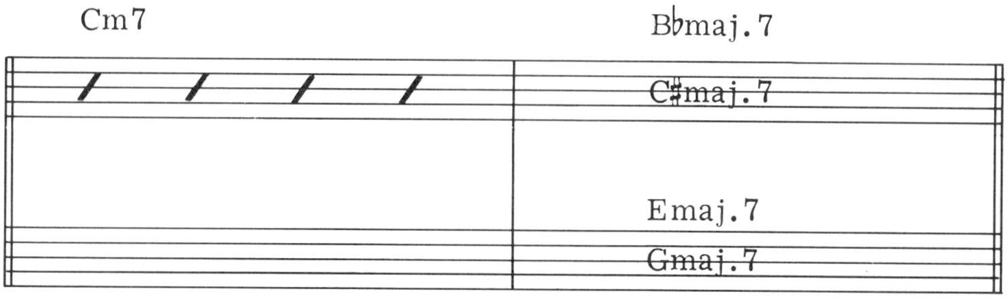

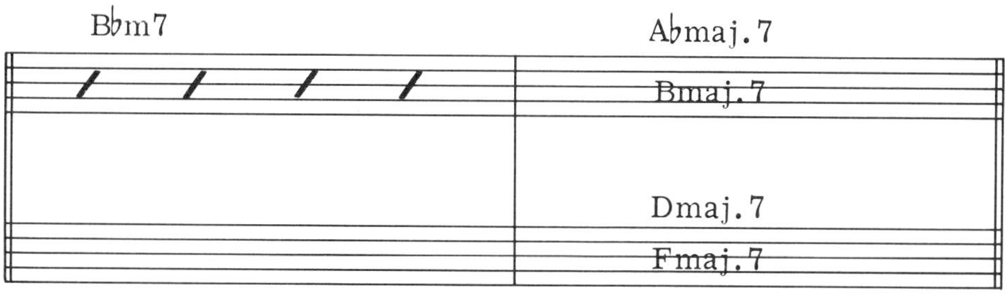

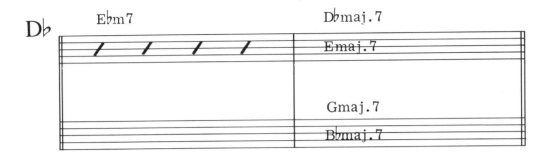

Try the 7th flat 9 in minor 3rds, and listen. You'll soon find out what sounds good (or someone will tell you). Try them in different places.

Practice dominant chords in the cycle of 4ths. Use these extensions.

9, 7b9, 7#9, 7b5, 7#5, 9b5, 9#5, 13, 13#5 13b5 13b9 13#9, 11, +7b9   +7
                                                                  (7#5b9) (7#5)

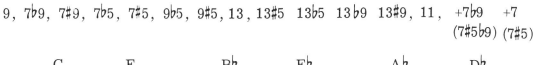

This small section is very important. It was written simply, so that it can be easily understood. The ability to move these chords smoothly is taken for granted by the professional player.

(2 - 5) progressions in the cycle of 4ths.

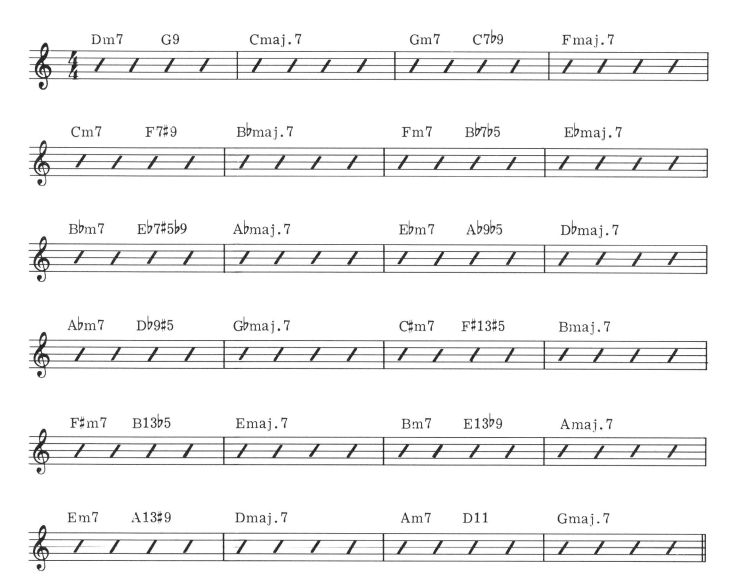

2 - 5 progressions leading from maj. 7 to minor 7th.

(using ♭5 of 5 substitute)

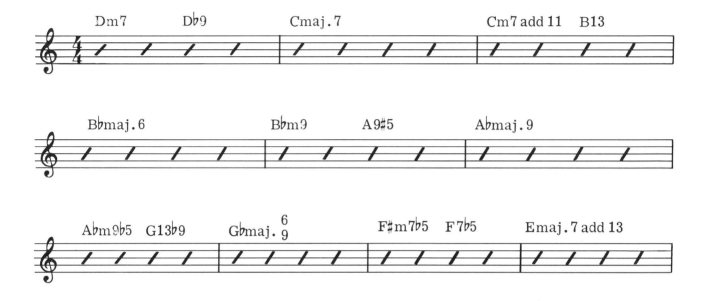

For turn-arounds and ending, other commonly used cycles can be used in place of 9ths.

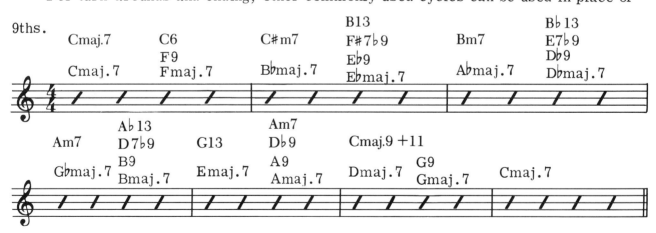

Minor 7th's in the cycle of 4ths.

Rule
At times the 4 major 7 or 4 dominant can be used for the one chord.

C

Cmaj.7 (can become) Cmaj.7 / Fmaj.7

Fmaj.7	Cmaj.7
F9	
Fmaj.7 Em7	Dm7 Cmaj.7
Cmaj.7 F13	Em7 Am7

F

Fmaj.7 / Fmaj.7 / Bbmaj.7

Bbmaj.7	Fmaj.7
Bb13	
Bbmaj.7 Am7	Gm7 Fmaj.7
Fmaj.7 Bb13	Am7 Dm7

Bb

Bbmaj.7 / Bbmaj.7 / Ebmaj.7

etc. ———→

Ebmaj.7 .	Bbmaj.7
Eb9	
Ebmaj.7 Dm7	Cm7 Bbmaj.7
Bbmaj.7 Eb13	Dm7 Gm7

Eb

Ebmaj.7 / Ebmaj.7 / Abmaj.7

Abmaj.7	Ebmaj.7
Abmaj.7 Gm7	Fm7 Ebmaj.7
Ebmaj.7 Ab13	Gm7 Cm7

Ab

Abmaj.7 / Abmaj.7 / Dbmaj.7

Dbmaj.7	Abmaj.7
Dbmaj.7 Cm7	Bbm7 Abmaj.7
Abmaj.7 Db13	Cm7 Fm7

Db

Dbmaj7 / Dbmaj.7 / Gbmaj.7

Gbmaj.7	Dbmaj.7
Gbmaj.7 Fm7	Ebm7 Bbmaj.7
Dbmaj.7 Gb13	Fm7 Bbm7

G♭

Measure 1: G♭maj.7 / / / / | Measure 2: (can became) / / / /

G♭maj.7	C♭maj.7
C♭maj.7	G♭maj.7
C♭maj.7 B♭m7	A♭m7 G♭maj.7
G♭maj.7 C♭13	B♭m7 E♭m7

B

Measure 1: Bmaj.7 / / / / | Measure 2: / / / /

Bmaj.7	Emaj.7
Emaj.7	Bmaj.7
Emaj.7 D♯m7	C♯m7 Bmaj.7
Bmaj.7 E13	D♯m7 G♯m7

E

Measure 1: Emaj.7 / / / / | Measure 2: / / / /

Emaj.7	Amaj.7
Amaj.7	Emaj.7
Amaj.7 G♯m7	F♯m7 Emaj.7
Emaj.7 A13	G♯m7 C♯m7

A

Measure 1: Amaj.7 / / / / | Measure 2: / / / /

Amaj.7	Dmaj.7
Dmaj.7	Amaj.7
Dmaj.7 C♯m7	Bm7 Amaj.7
Amaj.7 D13	C♯m7 F♯m7

D

Measure 1: Dmaj.7 / / / / | Measure 2: / / / /

Dmaj.7	Gmaj.7
Gmaj.7	Dmaj.7
Gmaj.7 F♯m7	Em7 Dmaj.7
Dmaj.7 G13	F♯m7 Bm7

G

Measure 1: Gmaj.7 / / / / | Measure 2: / / / /

Gmaj.7	Cmaj.7
Cmaj.7	Gmaj.7
Cmaj.7 Bm7	Am7 Gmaj.7
Gmaj.7 C13	Bm7 Em7

At times a dominant 7th chord can be used in place of a m7 using the same root, thereby enriching the Harmony - dom. 7th being the stronger chord.

Practice, listen, and learn—persistence pays off. In fact, it accounts for a lot of what is called talent. We haven't scratched the surface of music yet, but I hope you've enjoyed experimenting with these basic rules. Let your ear guide you to the substitutions that are most pleasing and accepted among jazz players. Applying all these rules should put you on a professional level. Remember, they apply to comping as well as soloing. Here are some of the most often played jazz chord progressions in their basic form, followed by the same chord progressions as they may be played by professionals. Peruse these and then try writing some improved changes to other tunes using these and the other rules as guidelines.

A good song writer is not necessarily a good musician. He may write great melodies but often sketchy chord changes. Any professional musician knows this and automatically reworks the tunes as follows. <u>Many options are included here—use your ears and edit accordingly—your own musical taste will govern which chords are right for you</u>. Don't try to use them all at once, clutter is tasteless. Comping is the art of flattering and inspiring the soloist. Play chord fills when the soloist is holding a note or resting. When he is playing lines, try to keep your chords in the middle register (or low) so that your top notes don't conflict with the solo lines. Use some enthusiasm to try to inspire the soloist. Think about how difficult it is for you to get inspired if the musician comping doesn't get enthusiastic or flatter you. Jazz is a sensitive exchange of feelings and ideas. Inspire each other! Remember feeling, compliment and feed each other!

Basic Chord Progression (example 1)

Basic

| Fm | B♭m | E♭7 | A♭ |

| D♭ | G7 | C | |

| Cm | Fm | B♭7 | E |

| A♭ | D7 | G | |

| D7 | | G | |

| Am6 | B7 | E | C+
C7 |

| Fm | B♭m | E♭7 | A♭ |

| D♭ | D♭m | A♭ | B° |

| E♭7 | | **1.** A♭ | |

| | | **2.** A♭ | |

60

Same progressions with substitutions and alterations.

Fm(9)
Fm7 Fm Fm(maj.7) Fm7 Fm6 | Bbm(9) / Bbm7 / Bbm Bbm(maj.7) Bbm7 Bbm6 | Eb9 Bbm7 / Ebm7 — Eb7b9 A13 | Abmaj.7 — Ab6 Ab13 / D9

Dbmaj.7 Db6/9 Dbmaj.7 | Dm7 G13 Db9 | Cmaj.7 Dm7 F9 | Em7 A13b9/A7b9 Dm7 Dbm7 G13b9/G7b9 Eb9 Dm7b5 Db9

Cm7 Cm11 Cm9 | Fm7 Fm11 Fm9 | Bb13 E9 | Eb6/9 E maj.9 Ebmaj.7 Eb6

Abmaj.7 Ab6 | Am7 D7b9 Ab13/Abmaj.7 | Gmaj.7 Am7 Cmaj.7/Cmaj.7b5 C13 | Bm7 E7b9 Bb13 E7b5 etc.

Am7 D9 | Am11 Ab7b5 | Gmaj.7 Am7 Am7 A#m7 | Bm7 Em7 Fm7

F#m7 F#m11 C13 | B13b9 B13 E9 | Emaj.7 6/9 Emaj.7 | Gm7b5b9 C+7b9

Fm9 Fm7 Fm(maj.7) Fm6 | Bbm9 Bbm7 Bbm(maj.7) Bbm6b | Ebsus Bbm7 Eb7b5 | Abmaj.7 Ab6 D9 / Ab7b9

Dbmaj.7 Bbm7 Db6/9 | Dbm7 Gb13 Dbm7 Gb9 Gb13sus Gb13 | Ab Cm7 Cm7 F9 | Bb7b9 Bm7 Bm7#5 E9 E7#9

Bbm7 Eb9 | Bbm7 Eb7b9(+11) Amaj.7 | **1.** Abmaj.9 Abm9 Ab6/Abm7 Abmaj.7 D7b5b9 | Gm9 Gm7b5 G7b5b9 Gm7 C+7#9 / C+7b9 / C13b9 C7b9/Gb13 C7b5b9

2. Abmaj.7 B13 Emaj.7 A+11 Amaj.7b5
Abmaj.7 Dbmaj.7 Gbmaj.7 Bmaj.7 | Emaj.7 Amaj.7 Abmaj.9

Add any alterations &
extensions to final chords.

Basic Chord Progression (example 2)

<u>Basic</u>

| F | A♭ | D♭ | B♭m7 |

| C7 | | F | |

| B♭m7 | E♭7 | A♭ | |

| Gm7 | C7 | F | Gm7   C7 |

| F | A♭ | D♭ | B♭m7 |

| C7 | | F | F7 |

| B♭ | C7   F | | A♭° |

| C7 | | ⌐1.⌐ F | Gm7   C7 |

| | | ⌐2.⌐ F | |

Same progression with substitutions and alterations.

Options

Fmaj.7 | Dm7 / Fm7 | Ebm7 / Db9 | Ab13 | Dbmaj.7 | | Gbmaj.7 | Gb6

Gm7 | C9 | Gm7 / Gb13 | C7b9 | Fmaj.7 Dm7 G7b9 | Cm7 | F7b9 / B13

Bbm7 | Eb9sus | Bbm11 / A7b5 / A13 | Eb7b9 / Eb7b5 | Abmaj.7 / Ab13 / Db9 | Ab6 | Dbmaj.7 / — | Bbm7 / Gbm7

— Mix them up! Play around with the turnarounds. —

Dm7 — Ab13 — G13 — Gb13
Am7 — D7b5 — Gm7 — C7b5
— D7b9 — — C7b9
Ab13 — Dbmaj.7 — Gb13
Abmaj.7 — Gm7 — Gbmaj.7

Gm7 | C13 | Gm7 / Gb7b9 / Gm7 Db9 | C13b9 / C9 C9+11 | | | |

Fmaj.7 / Fmaj.7 / (Gm7) | Fm7 / Fm7 Bb13b9 / (E9) | Ebm7 / D9 / Em7 A13 | Ab13 / Ab13 D9 | Dbmaj.7 | Db6 | Gbmaj.7 | Gb6

Gm7 | C13b9 / C9 | Gm7 | C7b5 b9 | Fmaj.7 | Dm7 G7b9 | Cm7 | F7b9

Bbmaj.7 | Am7 / D7#9 / (b5) | Gm7 | C9 | Am7 / Fmaj.7 | Dm7 / A7b9 Dm7 | G7b9 / G13 | Abm7 Db9 / G+7

Gm7 | C9 | Gm7 / Gb13 | C7b9 | 1. F6 / Fmaj.7 Dm7 | Ab7b9 | G7b9 / Gm7 | Gb7b9 / C7b9

Dm7 Ab13 G13 Abm7
Fmaj.7 A7b7 Dm7 G13
Gm7 Db9 C9 Gb7b9
Gbmaj.7

2. Eb9 Db9
Fmaj.7 Bb13 Ebmaj.7 Ab13 | Dbmaj.7 Gb13 Fmaj.9

Fmaj.7 Bbmaj.7 Eb maj.7 Ab maj.7 | Dbmaj.7 Gbmaj.7 F6/9+11

Fmaj.7 E7b9 Am7 D7b9 | Gm7 | Gbmaj.7 b5 Fmaj.9b b5

Blues

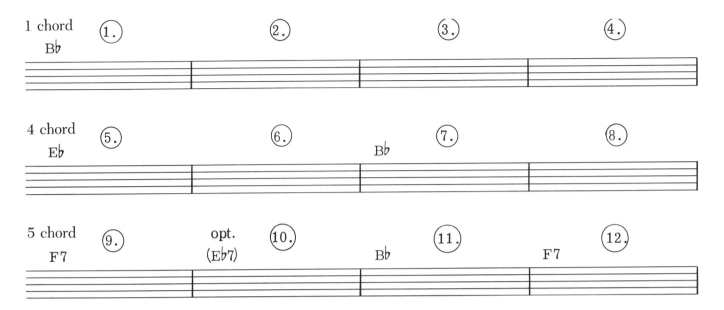

Blues Subs

Still basically 1–4–5

(1.) Bb6 / Bb13 E9 / Bm7(b5) E7b9 / Bbmaj.7 Fm7 Bb13 → / Bbmaj.7	(2.) ——Ab13—— / Eb9 / Eb9 B13 / Abm7 / → Am7 → D7b9 / → Ebmaj.7 / Am7 Abm7 / Cm7——— F9—	(3.) / Gm7 C7b9 / Bbmaj.7 Cm7 / Gbm7 / → Gm7 → C7b9 / → Dm7 Cm7(F7b9) / Gm7 Gbm7	(4.) Fm7 B13 Bb13 E9 / Fm7 Bb13b9 / E9 / → Fm7 → Bb7b9 / Bm7 E9 / Fm7 E9
(5.) Eb9 / Eb9 / Ebmaj.7 / Eb9	(6.) Ebm7 Ab13 / Eb9 Bb° / B13 / Ebm7 Ab13 / Em7 → A13	(7.) Dm7 G13 / Bb13 A13 / Bbmaj.7 Cm7 / Bb13 A7b9 / Abm7 Db9 / Dm7 G13 / → B 13	(8.) Dbm7 Gb13 / Ab13 G13b9 / Dm7 Dbm7 / Dm7 G7b9 / Dbm7 Gb13 / Dbm7 Gb13
(9.) Gm7 / Dm7 G7b9 / Cm7 F9 / F13 / Cm7 F13 / Gm7 C9	(10.) C9(13) / Cm7 Bmaj.7 / Cm7 F7b9 / F#m7 B13 / Cm7 F13b9	(11.) Gm7 C7b9 / Bbmaj.7 Gm7 / Dm7 G7b9 / Dm7 Db9 / Dm7 Dbm7 / Bbmaj.7 Db13(b9) / Bbmaj.7 Abm7 Db9 / ——Db maj.7——	(12.) Cm7 F9b9 / B13 / Cm11 B7b5 / Cm7 B9+11 / C13(b9) B13(b9) / G maj.7 B9+11 / —Gmaj.7—

These are some typical options for the Jazz Blues.
Combine them with each other to make unlimited variations.
Again, use your ears be experimental but sensitive.

For All Instruments
THE JAZZ PLAYER'S HANDBOOK
EXTENSIONS AND ALTERATIONS

RULE 1:

A jazz player never uses a plain major chord or a plain dominant 7th except for effect.

A <u>C Major chord</u> can become: C6, C Major 7, C Major 6 add 9, C Major 9, C Major 7 b5, C Major 7 aug. 11, C Major 7 add. 13, C Major 7 #5, C Major 7 add. 6 add. 9, C Major 9 b5, C Major 9 #11, C Major 7 #9 #11, C Major 7 b5 b9, etc.

A <u>C Minor Chord</u> can become: Cm6, Cm add (major 7), Cm add. 9, Cm (add. major 7 add. 9), Cm b5, Cm (major 7) b5, Cm#11, Cm#11 (add. major 7), Cm6 (add. major 7), Cm#5, Cm6 add. 9, etc.

The <u>C dominant</u> chords become: C9, C11, C13, C7b9, C7#9, C7b5, C7#5, C7#5b9, C7b5#9, C7#5#9, C7b5b9, C9b5, C9+11, C13 add. 11, C13b9, C13#9, C7sus. 4, C9sus.4, C13b5, C+7, C+7b9, C+7add9, C+7#9, etc.

SUBSTITUTIONS

RULE 1:

Diminished chords become 7thb9 chords by using them over a root a half-tone lower than any note in the chord. Each diminished chord provides 4 7thb9 chords. Taste will decide the choice.

Example: <u>C diminished chord</u> (o)

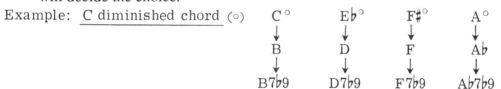

The Major scale is harmonized in four note chords. For purposes of substituting and transposing, that harmonized scale should be memorized by chord names and numbers.

Example: Key of C Major – Transpose to all keys.

[Bø7]

CMaj7	Dm7	Em7	FMaj7	G7	Am7	Bm7b5	C maj.7
1	2	3	4	5	6	7	8/1
8							

RULE 2:

(3) minor 7th Chords and (6) minor 7th chords = the (1) Major chord.

Example: Em7 + Am7 = CMajor7

RULE 3:

The 5 minor 7th of a dominant 7th chord can be used before, after, or in place of the dominant 7th chord.

	before		after		in place of
Example:	Dm7 = G7		G7—Dm		Dm7
	2 5		5 2		2

RULE 4:

When the (2) minor 7th chord is placed before the (5) dominant 7th chord, a 2-5 chord progression is created.

Example: Dm7   G9   CMajor7

   (2)   -   (5)   -   (1)

Bass line moves in 4ths
  (D-G-C)

RULE 5:

When C four beats and G7 four beats is found, combining rules 3 and 4 will give you the very common 1, 6, 2, 5 progression.

Example: CMajor7   Am7   Dm7   G9
    1   -   6   -   2   -   5

A variation on this is the 1, 3, 2, 5.

Example: CMajor7   Em7   Dm7   G9
    1   -   3   -   2   -   5

RULE 6:

The flat (5) dominant 7 chord of the dominant 7th chord can be used in place of the 5 dominant 7th.

Example: G7   (to)   CMajor7
    (5)   (1)

V.S.

$$5 \quad \text{of } 5 = \begin{array}{ccccc} G & A & B & C & \boxed{D} \\ 1 & 2 & 3 & 4 & 5 \end{array}$$

add a flat to create the D♭9
    flat 5 of 5

| D♭9 | to | CMajor7 |

D♭ dominant is the flat 5 substitute of G dominant. This is also called a tri tone sub—the

tri tone being achieved by counting up 3 whole tones from the root—

$$\begin{array}{ccc} 1 & 2 & 3 \\ \multicolumn{3}{c}{\text{C-D-E-F\#}} \\ \multicolumn{3}{c}{\text{G♭}} \end{array}$$

| Dm7 | D♭9 | CMajor7 |

Bass line moves chromatically   (D-D♭-C)

RULE 7:

A minor 6th chord leading to a dominant 7th chord one whole root tone above (Gm6 to A7♭9) is misspelled. It should be (5) minor 7th ♭5 of the dominant 7.

Example: (Gm6 to A7♭9) should be Em7♭5 to A7♭9.

Gm6 and Em7♭5 have the same notes but a different root.

RULE 8:

When leading to a minor type chord, always alter the dominant 7th before it.

Example: (G9 to Cm)
        G7♭9 to Cm, G7♯9 to Cm, G+7(G7♯5) to Cm etc.

Remember to combine rules. Always play all of your choices, then decide on the ones you like. Keep the melody in mind and use your ear!!

Remember that any chord with a flat 7 in it is a leading chord and any chord with a major 7 (natural 7) stops the harmony. The (2) m7 or (5) dom 7th determine your tonal centers. They both lead to 1 which is your tonal center.

Example: Dm7, G13 bring you to C Major (C minor).

Many chords have the same notes and become different when used with different bass notes or placed in progressions in different ways.

Example: G6 and Em7 are the same chord.
        GMajor9 and Bminor7 are the same chord.
        Gm6 can be C9, Em7♭5, G♭+7♭9, B♭6♭5, D♭9, can be E♭9 sus.

    A minor 11 (no 3rd) can be used for D11 or D sus.

    C7♭5 can be used for C7+11 or G♭7+11.

    Gmin. 9 = B♭ maj.7

    Gm maj.7 = G♭+, D+, B+

    Gm6 =   C9

        Em7♭5

        etc. These are but a few examples. Try to find more. They are

        useful for improvising.

The difference is in what the chord is moving to, or what is being used in the bass.

Minor third intervals also play an important role in substituting.

Example: C7, E♭7, G♭7, A7 can all lead to F major.

RULE 9:

Dom. 7th chords a minor 3rd apart sub for each other.

The same holds true for minor 7th chords.

Example: Gm7, B♭m7, D♭m7, Em7 all can lead to F.

Also Major 7th chords can move in minor 3rds.

Example: Gm7 leads to Fmajor7, A♭major7, Bmajor7, Dmajor7.

Try 7th♭9 chords in minor 3rds and listen. You'll soon find out what sounds good.

Play dominant chords in the cycle of 4ths. Then play 2 - 5 progressions in the cycle. Use major 7ths in place of some or all of the dominant 7ths in the cycle of 4ths for resolutions, etc.

RULE 10:

At times the (4) major 7 or (4) dominant can be used for the one chord.

Example: Fmajor7 or F9 in place of Cmajor7.

RULE 11:

At times a minor 7th can be made into a dominant 7th using the same root.

For thorough knowledge, everything should be practiced in the cycle of 4ths. It'll take a while, but it will certainly be worth it. There should be no favorite key. They're all musical and should be used as such.

All of these rules apply to the scales and arpeggios for improvising as well as chord playing.